FAX
THIS BOOK

**OVER 100 SIT-UP-AND-TAKE-NOTICE
COVER SHEETS FOR BETTER BUSINESS**

BY JOHN CALDWELL

WORKMAN PUBLISHING, NEW YORK

ACKNOWLEDGMENTS

Many thanks to my good friend Frank Visco, who insisted that I do a book of fax cover pages. Thanks for the idea, Frank. Now don't just sit there—what do I do next?!

And special thanks to Sally Kovalchick, Julie Hansen, Lisa Hollander and everyone else at Workman Publishing, who helped turn my scrawls into this book.

Library of Congress Cataloging-in-Publication Data

Caldwell, John, 1946–
Fax this book : over 100 sit-up-and-take-notice cover sheets for better business… / by John Caldwell.
p. cm.
ISBN 0-89480-807-9
1. Commercial correspondence–Caricatures and cartoons. 2. Facsimile transmission. I. Title.
HF5726.C18 1990 90-11963
651.7′5–dc20 CIP

Workman books are available at special discounts when purchased in bulk for premiums and sales promotions as well as for fund-raising or educational use.
Special editions or book excerpts can also be created to specification. For details, contact the Special Sales Director at the address below.

Workman Publishing Company, Inc.
708 Broadway
New York, NY 10003

Manufactured in the United States of America

First printing May 1990

15 14 13 12 11 10

Contents

To Whom It May Concern

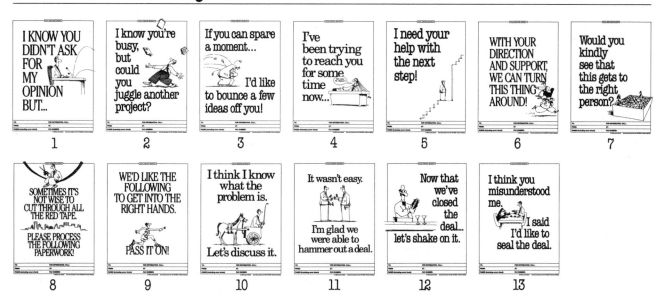
Memos & Reports

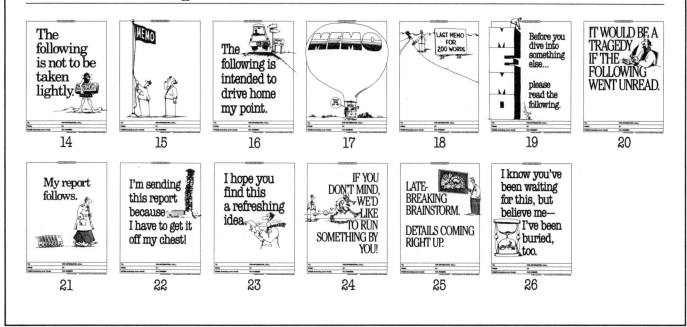

Over to You

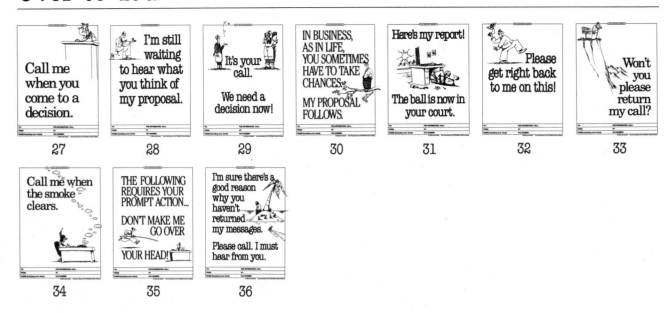

27 — Call me when you come to a decision.

28 — I'm still waiting to hear what you think of my proposal.

29 — It's your call. We need a decision now!

30 — IN BUSINESS, AS IN LIFE, YOU SOMETIMES HAVE TO TAKE CHANCES. MY PROPOSAL FOLLOWS.

31 — Here's my report! The ball is now in your court.

32 — Please get right back to me on this!

33 — Won't you please return my call?

34 — Call me when the smoke clears.

35 — THE FOLLOWING REQUIRES YOUR PROMPT ACTION... DON'T MAKE ME GO OVER YOUR HEAD!

36 — I'm sure there's a good reason why you haven't returned my messages. Please call. I must hear from you.

Let's Meet

37 — Would you pencil me in? I'd like to meet with you!

38 — I realize you don't know me from Adam... but I'd like to make an appointment to stop by.

39 — If you can squeeze me in, I'd like to drop by and discuss the following...

40 — IT'S IMPORTANT TO KEEP THINGS IN PERSPECTIVE.... LET'S SET UP A MEETING!

41 — If we get together, I'm sure we can iron out our differences.

42 — Perhaps you don't understand the gravity of the situation! We need to meet.

43 — Before this problem gets any bigger.... I think we should schedule a meeting!

44 — Remember that idea we put on the back burner? I think we need to discuss it!

45 — Our meeting wouldn't be complete without you. Please attend.

46 — You just can't get a power lunch started alone. Care to join me?

47 — EMERGENCY!!! Let's meet for lunch!

48 — I DON'T WANT TO MAKE A BIG PRODUCTION OUT OF THIS, BUT I THINK WE SHOULD MEET FOR LUNCH!

Nuts & Bolts

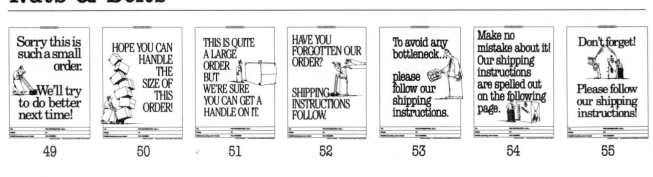

49 — Sorry this is such a small order. We'll try to do better next time!

50 — HOPE YOU CAN HANDLE THE SIZE OF THIS ORDER!

51 — THIS IS QUITE A LARGE ORDER BUT WE'RE SURE YOU CAN GET A HANDLE ON IT.

52 — HAVE YOU FORGOTTEN OUR ORDER? SHIPPING INSTRUCTIONS FOLLOW.

53 — To avoid any bottleneck. please follow our shipping instructions.

54 — Make no mistake about it! Our shipping instructions are spelled out on the following page.

55 — Don't forget! Please follow our shipping instructions!

56 — It took some labor but here's your proof of delivery.

57 — Elementary! We've tracked down your proof of delivery.

58 — HERE'S OUR BILL. PLEASE LOOK IT OVER CAREFULLY

59 — Coming up: One educated guesstimate.

60 — Sure, it's a mess! But we can lick your problem. Here's our estimate.

61 — It's a whale of a job. Here's our estimate.

Money Matters

62 — Just a reminder. you owe us some money!

63 — According to our books your payment is late!

64 — We've gone through this before. According to our books you still owe us money!

65 — Cash flow problems can keep you hopping, but we'd still like you to pay your bill!

66 — WE'RE GETTING DESPERATE! PLEASE DROP US, A CHECK!

67 — We'd appreciate it if you'd dig a little deeper and come up with the money you owe us!

68 — Is this any way to leave us? Please pay your bill.

69 — AFTER SWALLOWING YOUR EXCUSES, WE HAVE ONLY TWO WORDS TO SAY: CHECK PLEASE!

70 — According to our records, you still owe us money.

71 — If your payment is on it's way, please disregard this transmission!

72 — Give yourself some credit. Fill out our form.

73 — Everything we are today, we owe to people like you. If you'd like to owe us something, please fill out the enclosed credit form.

74 — You're okay in our book. Your credit has been approved.

75 — And now for the damage. Our invoice follows!

Oops!

76 — To err is human... to forgive is good business!

77 — Sorry this took so long.

78 — Sorry I missed your call. I was having an out-of-office experience.

79 — I'VE PUT MY FINGER ON THE PROBLEM. SORRY, IT WON'T HAPPEN AGAIN.

80 — SORRY! OUR COMPUTER IS PLAYING TRICKS ON US.

81 — At the present time, our computers are not operating at peak efficiency.

82 — #@✻☆٭!! COMPUTERS! THEY'VE DONE IT AGAIN!

How Are We Doing?

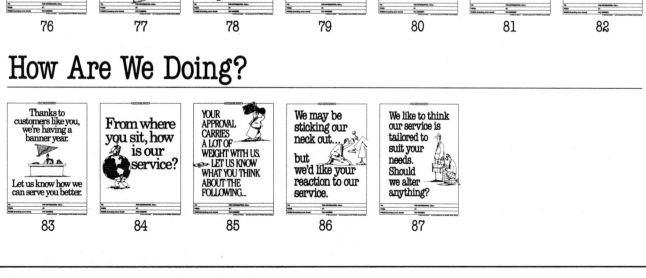

83 — Thanks to customers like you, we're having a banner year. Let us know how we can serve you better.

84 — From where you sit, how is our service?

85 — YOUR APPROVAL CARRIES A LOT OF WEIGHT WITH US. LET US KNOW WHAT YOU THINK ABOUT THE FOLLOWING...

86 — We may be sticking our neck out... but we'd like your reaction to our service.

87 — We like to think our service is tailored to suit your needs. Should we alter anything?

Congratulations

88   89   90   91   92

Etc.

93   94   95   96   97   98   99

100   101

I KNOW YOU DIDN'T ASK FOR MY OPINION BUT...

TO:

FOR INFORMATION, CALL:

FROM:

AT:

PAGES (including cover sheet):

FAX NUMBER:

I know you're busy, but could you juggle another project?

TO:	**FOR INFORMATION, CALL:**
FROM:	**AT:**
PAGES (including cover sheet):	**FAX NUMBER:**

If you can spare a moment...

I'd like to bounce a few ideas off you!

TO:	FOR INFORMATION, CALL:
FROM:	AT:
PAGES (including cover sheet):	FAX NUMBER:

I've been trying to reach you for some time now...

ANY LUCK, MS. MUFFET?

TO: **FOR INFORMATION, CALL:**

FROM: **AT:**

PAGES (including cover sheet):   **FAX NUMBER:**

I need your help with the next step!

TO:	**FOR INFORMATION, CALL:**
FROM:	**AT:**
PAGES (including cover sheet):	**FAX NUMBER:**

WITH YOUR DIRECTION AND SUPPORT, WE CAN TURN THIS THING AROUND!

TO:

FROM:

PAGES (including cover sheet):

FOR INFORMATION, CALL:

AT:

FAX NUMBER:

Would you kindly see that this gets to the right person?

TO:

FOR INFORMATION, CALL:

FROM:

AT:

PAGES (including cover sheet):

FAX NUMBER:

SOMETIMES IT'S NOT WISE TO CUT THROUGH ALL THE RED TAPE.

PLEASE PROCESS THE FOLLOWING PAPERWORK!

TO: **FOR INFORMATION, CALL:**

FROM: **AT:**

PAGES (including cover sheet):   **FAX NUMBER:**

WE'D LIKE THE FOLLOWING TO GET INTO THE RIGHT HANDS.

PASS IT ON!

TO:

FOR INFORMATION, CALL:

FROM:

AT:

PAGES (including cover sheet):

FAX NUMBER:

I think I know what the problem is.

Let's discuss it.

TO:	**FOR INFORMATION, CALL:**
FROM:	**AT:**
PAGES (including cover sheet):	**FAX NUMBER:**

It wasn't easy.

I'm glad we were able to hammer out a deal.

TO:	**FOR INFORMATION, CALL:**
FROM:	**AT:**
PAGES (including cover sheet):	**FAX NUMBER:**

Now that we've closed the deal...

let's shake on it.

TO:

FROM:

PAGES (including cover sheet):

FOR INFORMATION, CALL:

AT:

FAX NUMBER:

I think you misunderstood me.

I said I'd like to seal the deal.

TO:

FOR INFORMATION, CALL:

FROM:

AT:

PAGES (including cover sheet):

FAX NUMBER:

The following is not to be taken lightly.

TO:

FROM:

PAGES (including cover sheet):

FOR INFORMATION, CALL:

AT:

FAX NUMBER:

TO:

FROM:

PAGES (including cover sheet):

FOR INFORMATION, CALL:

AT:

FAX NUMBER:

The following is intended to drive home my point.

TO: **FOR INFORMATION, CALL:**

FROM: **AT:**

PAGES (including cover sheet):   **FAX NUMBER:**

TO:

FROM:

PAGES (including cover sheet):

FOR INFORMATION, CALL:

AT:

FAX NUMBER:

TO:

FOR INFORMATION, CALL:

FROM:

AT:

PAGES (including cover sheet):

FAX NUMBER:

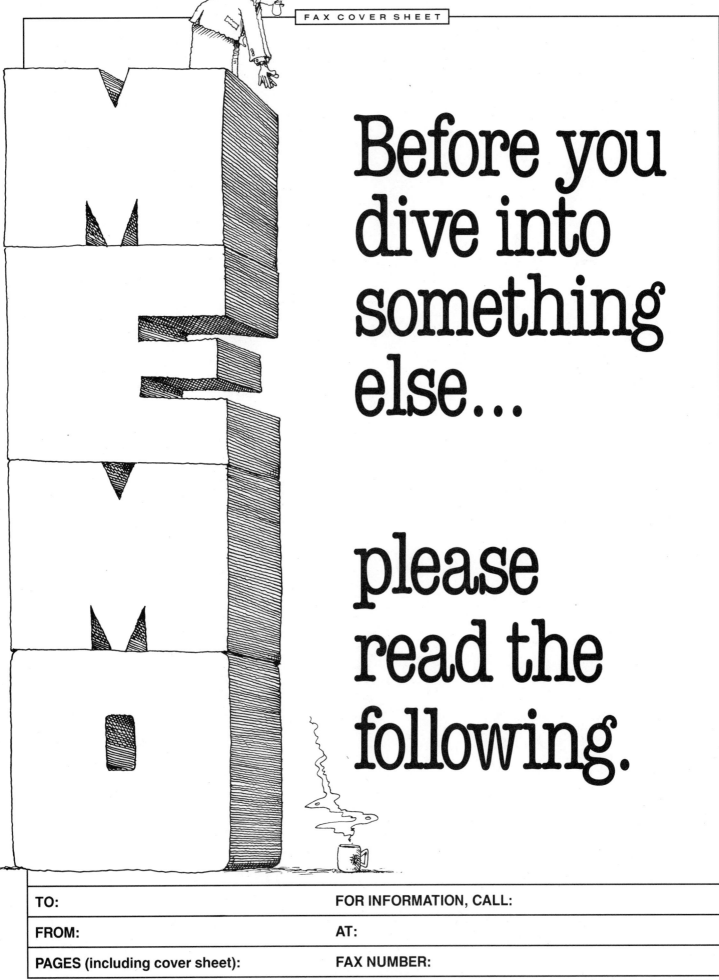

Before you dive into something else...

please read the following.

TO:	**FOR INFORMATION, CALL:**
FROM:	**AT:**
PAGES (including cover sheet):	**FAX NUMBER:**

IT WOULD BE A TRAGEDY IF THE FOLLOWING WENT UNREAD.

MEMO:

TO:

FOR INFORMATION, CALL:

FROM:

AT:

PAGES (including cover sheet):

FAX NUMBER:

My report follows.

TO:

FROM:

PAGES (including cover sheet):

FOR INFORMATION, CALL:

AT:

FAX NUMBER:

I'm sending this report because I have to get it off my chest!

TO:	**FOR INFORMATION, CALL:**
FROM:	**AT:**
PAGES (including cover sheet):	**FAX NUMBER:**

I hope you find this a refreshing idea.

TO:	FOR INFORMATION, CALL:
FROM:	AT:
PAGES (including cover sheet):	FAX NUMBER:

IF YOU DON'T MIND, WE'D LIKE TO RUN SOMETHING BY YOU!

TO: **FOR INFORMATION, CALL:**

FROM: **AT:**

PAGES (including cover sheet):   **FAX NUMBER:**

PAGES (including cover sheet):

LATE-BREAKING BRAINSTORM.

DETAILS COMING RIGHT UP.

TO: FOR INFORMATION, CALL:

FROM: AT:

PAGES (including cover sheet):   FAX NUMBER:

I know you've been waiting for this, but believe me— I've been buried, too.

TO:

FROM:

PAGES (including cover sheet):

FOR INFORMATION, CALL:

AT:

FAX NUMBER:

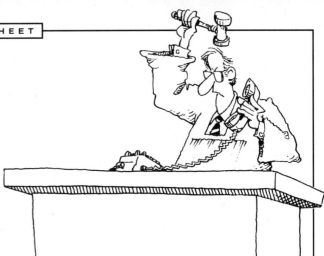

Call me when you come to a decision.

TO:	**FOR INFORMATION, CALL:**
FROM:	**AT:**
PAGES (including cover sheet):	**FAX NUMBER:**

I'm still waiting to hear what you think of my proposal.

TO:	FOR INFORMATION, CALL:
FROM:	AT:
PAGES (including cover sheet):	FAX NUMBER:

It's your call.

We need a decision now!

TO:	**FOR INFORMATION, CALL:**
FROM:	**AT:**
PAGES (including cover sheet):	**FAX NUMBER:**

IN BUSINESS, AS IN LIFE, YOU SOMETIMES HAVE TO TAKE CHANCES.

MY PROPOSAL FOLLOWS.

TO:

FROM:

PAGES (including cover sheet):

FOR INFORMATION, CALL:

AT:

FAX NUMBER:

Here's my report!

The ball is now in your court.

TO:	**FOR INFORMATION, CALL:**
FROM:	**AT:**
PAGES (including cover sheet):	**FAX NUMBER:**

Please get right back to me on this!

TO:	FOR INFORMATION, CALL:
FROM:	AT:
PAGES (including cover sheet):	FAX NUMBER:

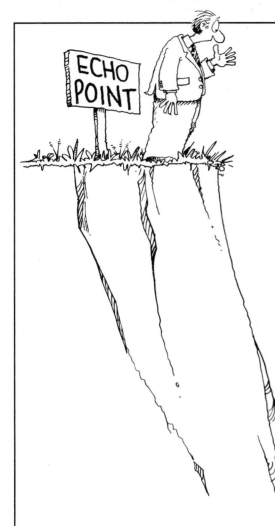

ECHO POINT

Won't you please return my call?

TO:	FOR INFORMATION, CALL:
FROM:	AT:
PAGES (including cover sheet):	FAX NUMBER:

Call me when the smoke clears.

TO:

FOR INFORMATION, CALL:

FROM:

AT:

PAGES (including cover sheet):

FAX NUMBER:

THE FOLLOWING REQUIRES YOUR PROMPT ACTION...

DON'T MAKE ME GO OVER

YOUR HEAD!

TO:	**FOR INFORMATION, CALL:**
FROM:	**AT:**
PAGES (including cover sheet):	**FAX NUMBER:**

I'm sure there's a good reason why you haven't returned my messages.

Please call. I must hear from you.

TO:

FOR INFORMATION, CALL:

FROM:

AT:

PAGES (including cover sheet):

FAX NUMBER:

Would you pencil me in?

I'd like to meet with you!

TO:	FOR INFORMATION, CALL:
FROM:	AT:
PAGES (including cover sheet):	FAX NUMBER:

I realize you don't know me from Adam... but I'd like to make an appointment to stop by.

TO:	**FOR INFORMATION, CALL:**
FROM:	**AT:**
PAGES (including cover sheet):	**FAX NUMBER:**

If you can squeeze me in,

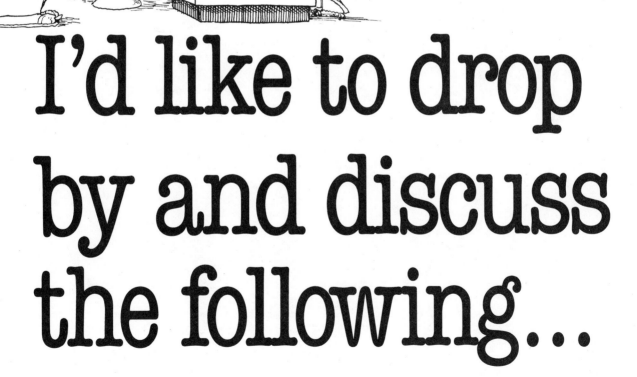

I'd like to drop by and discuss the following...

TO:

FOR INFORMATION, CALL:

FROM:

AT:

PAGES (including cover sheet):

FAX NUMBER:

IT'S IMPORTANT TO KEEP THINGS IN PERSPECTIVE...

LET'S SET UP A MEETING!

TO:	FOR INFORMATION, CALL:
FROM:	AT:
PAGES (including cover sheet):	FAX NUMBER:

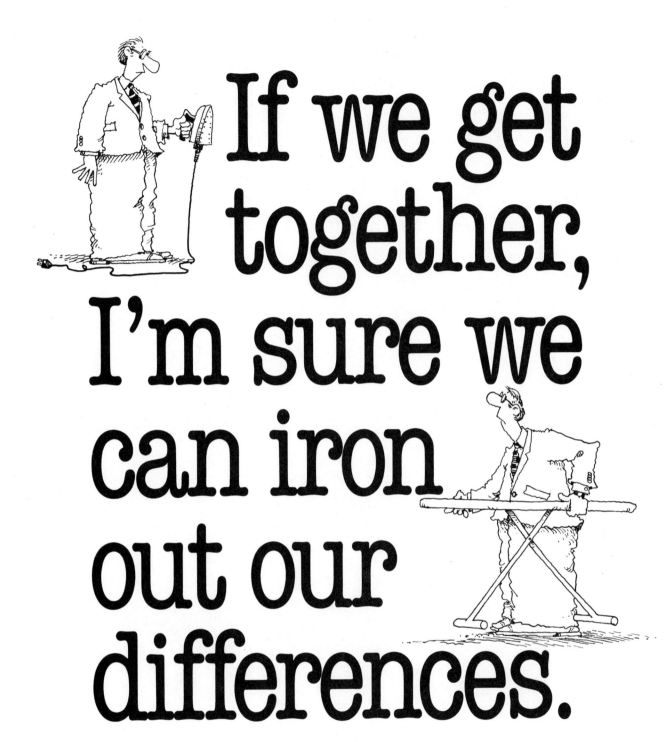

If we get together, I'm sure we can iron out our differences.

TO:	**FOR INFORMATION, CALL:**
FROM:	**AT:**
PAGES (including cover sheet):	**FAX NUMBER:**

Perhaps you don't understand the gravity of the situation!

We need to meet.

TO:	FOR INFORMATION, CALL:
FROM:	AT:
PAGES (including cover sheet):	FAX NUMBER:

Before this problem gets any bigger...

I think we should schedule a meeting!

TO:	**FOR INFORMATION, CALL:**
FROM:	**AT:**
PAGES (including cover sheet):	**FAX NUMBER:**

Remember that idea we put on the back burner?

I think we need to discuss it!

TO:	FOR INFORMATION, CALL:
FROM:	AT:
PAGES (including cover sheet):	FAX NUMBER:

Our meeting wouldn't be complete without you.

Please attend.

TO:	**FOR INFORMATION, CALL:**
FROM:	**AT:**
PAGES (including cover sheet):	**FAX NUMBER:**

You just can't get a power lunch started alone.

Care to join me?

TO: FOR INFORMATION, CALL:

FROM: AT:

PAGES (including cover sheet):   FAX NUMBER:

EMERGENCY!!!

LET ME THROUGH, PLEASE! I'M AN MBA!

Let's meet for lunch!

TO:	**FOR INFORMATION, CALL:**
FROM:	**AT:**
PAGES (including cover sheet):	**FAX NUMBER:**

I DON'T WANT TO MAKE A BIG PRODUCTION OUT OF THIS, BUT I THINK WE SHOULD MEET FOR LUNCH!

TO:

FROM:

PAGES (including cover sheet):

FOR INFORMATION, CALL:

AT:

FAX NUMBER:

Sorry this is such a small order. We'll try to do better next time!

TO:	**FOR INFORMATION, CALL:**
FROM:	**AT:**
PAGES (including cover sheet):	**FAX NUMBER:**

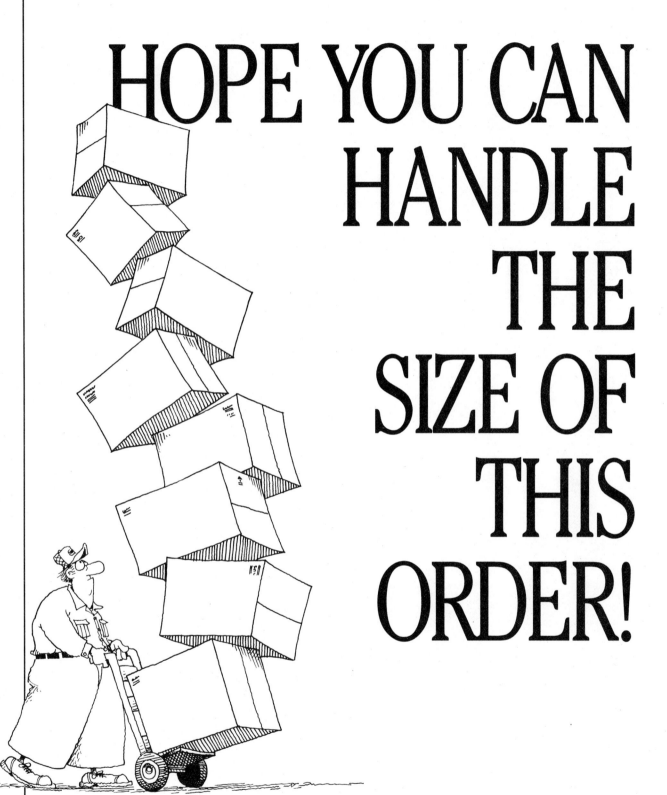

HOPE YOU CAN HANDLE THE SIZE OF THIS ORDER!

TO: **FOR INFORMATION, CALL:**

FROM: **AT:**

PAGES (including cover sheet):   **FAX NUMBER:**

THIS IS QUITE A LARGE ORDER BUT WE'RE SURE YOU CAN GET A HANDLE ON IT.

TO:

FOR INFORMATION, CALL:

FROM:

AT:

PAGES (including cover sheet):

FAX NUMBER:

HAVE YOU FORGOTTEN OUR ORDER?

SHIPPING INSTRUCTIONS FOLLOW.

TO: **FOR INFORMATION, CALL:**

FROM: **AT:**

PAGES (including cover sheet):   **FAX NUMBER:**

To avoid any bottleneck...

please follow our shipping instructions.

TO:

FOR INFORMATION, CALL:

FROM:

AT:

PAGES (including cover sheet):

FAX NUMBER:

Make no mistake about it! Our shipping instructions are spelled out on the following page.

RUSH ODER!

THIS SYDE UP!

FRAJILE!

HANDEL WITH KARE!

TO:

FROM:

PAGES (including cover sheet):

FOR INFORMATION, CALL:

AT:

FAX NUMBER:

Don't forget!

THIS END UP

Please follow our shipping instructions!

TO:	FOR INFORMATION, CALL:
FROM:	AT:
PAGES (including cover sheet):	FAX NUMBER:

It took some labor but here's your proof of delivery.

TO:

FROM:

PAGES (including cover sheet):

FOR INFORMATION, CALL:

AT:

FAX NUMBER:

Elementary!

We've tracked down your proof of delivery.

TO:	FOR INFORMATION, CALL:
FROM:	AT:
PAGES (including cover sheet):	FAX NUMBER:

HERE'S OUR BILL. PLEASE LOOK IT OVER CAREFULLY.

TO:	**FOR INFORMATION, CALL:**
FROM:	**AT:**
PAGES (including cover sheet):	**FAX NUMBER:**

Coming up:

One educated guesstimate.

TO:	**FOR INFORMATION, CALL:**
FROM:	**AT:**
PAGES (including cover sheet):	**FAX NUMBER:**

Sure, it's a mess! But we can lick your problem.

Here's our estimate.

TO:	FOR INFORMATION, CALL:
FROM:	AT:
PAGES (including cover sheet):	FAX NUMBER:

It's a whale of a job. Here's our estimate.

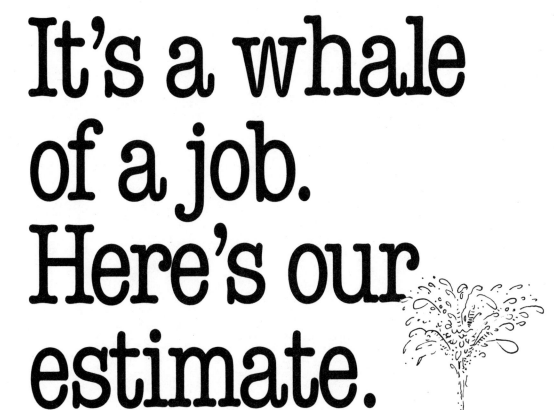

TO:	FOR INFORMATION, CALL:
FROM:	AT:
PAGES (including cover sheet):	FAX NUMBER:

Just a reminder...

you owe us some money!

TO:

FOR INFORMATION, CALL:

FROM:

AT:

PAGES (including cover sheet):

FAX NUMBER:

According to our books

your payment is late!

TO:

FROM:

PAGES (including cover sheet):

FOR INFORMATION, CALL:

AT:

FAX NUMBER:

We've gone through this before.

According to our books you still owe us money!

TO: **FOR INFORMATION, CALL:**

FROM: **AT:**

PAGES (including cover sheet):   **FAX NUMBER:**

Cash flow problems can keep you hopping, but we'd still like you to pay your bill!

TO:

FOR INFORMATION, CALL:

FROM:

AT:

PAGES (including cover sheet):

FAX NUMBER:

WE'RE GETTING DESPERATE!

PLEASE DROP US A CHECK!

TO:

FOR INFORMATION, CALL:

FROM:

AT:

PAGES (including cover sheet):

FAX NUMBER:

We'd appreciate it if you'd dig a little deeper and come up with the money you owe us!

TO:

FOR INFORMATION, CALL:

FROM:

AT:

PAGES (including cover sheet):

FAX NUMBER:

Is this any way to leave us?

Please pay your bill.

TO: **FOR INFORMATION, CALL:**

FROM: **AT:**

PAGES (including cover sheet):   **FAX NUMBER:**

AFTER SWALLOWING YOUR EXCUSES, WE HAVE ONLY TWO WORDS TO SAY:

TO: | **FOR INFORMATION, CALL:**

FROM: | **AT:**

PAGES (including cover sheet): | **FAX NUMBER:**

According to our records, you still owe us money.

THIS IS YOUR VINYL NOTICE!

TO: **FOR INFORMATION, CALL:**

FROM: **AT:**

PAGES (including cover sheet):   **FAX NUMBER:**

If your payment is on its way, please disregard this transmission!

TO:

FOR INFORMATION, CALL:

FROM:

AT:

PAGES (including cover sheet):

FAX NUMBER:

Give yourself some credit.

PAT PAT PAT

Fill out our form.

TO:	**FOR INFORMATION, CALL:**
FROM:	**AT:**
PAGES (including cover sheet):	**FAX NUMBER:**

Everything we are today, we owe to people like you.

If you'd like to owe us something, please fill out the enclosed credit form.

TO:	FOR INFORMATION, CALL:
FROM:	AT:
PAGES (including cover sheet):	FAX NUMBER:

You're okay in our book. Your credit has been approved.

TO:	FOR INFORMATION, CALL:
FROM:	AT:
PAGES (including cover sheet):	FAX NUMBER:

And now for the damage.

Our invoice follows!

TO:	FOR INFORMATION, CALL:
FROM:	AT:
PAGES (including cover sheet):	FAX NUMBER:

To err is human...

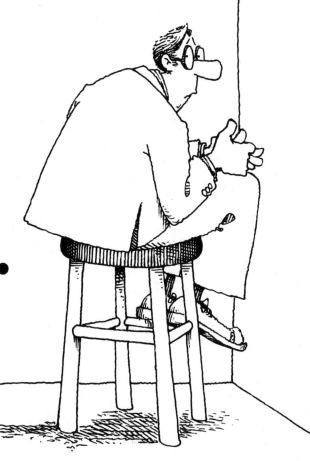

to forgive is good business!

TO: **FOR INFORMATION, CALL:**

FROM: **AT:**

PAGES (including cover sheet):   **FAX NUMBER:**

Sorry this took so long.

TO:

FROM:

PAGES (including cover sheet):

FOR INFORMATION, CALL:

AT:

FAX NUMBER:

Sorry I missed your call. I was having an out-of-office experience.

TO:

FOR INFORMATION, CALL:

FROM:

AT:

PAGES (including cover sheet):

FAX NUMBER:

I'VE PUT MY FINGER ON THE PROBLEM.

SORRY, IT WON'T HAPPEN AGAIN.

TO:

FOR INFORMATION, CALL:

FROM:

AT:

PAGES (including cover sheet):

FAX NUMBER:

SORRY!

OUR COMPUTER IS PLAYING TRICKS ON US.

TO:

FROM:

PAGES (including cover sheet):

FOR INFORMATION, CALL:

AT:

FAX NUMBER:

At the present time, our computers are not operating at peak efficiency.

TO:

FROM:

PAGES (including cover sheet):

FOR INFORMATION, CALL:

AT:

FAX NUMBER:

COMPUTERS!

THEY'VE DONE IT AGAIN!

TO:	FOR INFORMATION, CALL:
FROM:	AT:
PAGES (including cover sheet):	FAX NUMBER:

Thanks to customers like you, we're having a banner year.

Let us know how we can serve you better.

TO:	FOR INFORMATION, CALL:
FROM:	AT:
PAGES (including cover sheet):	FAX NUMBER:

From where you sit, how is our service?

TO:

FROM:

PAGES (including cover sheet):

FOR INFORMATION, CALL:

AT:

FAX NUMBER:

YOUR APPROVAL CARRIES A LOT OF WEIGHT WITH US. LET US KNOW WHAT YOU THINK ABOUT THE FOLLOWING...

TO:

FROM:

PAGES (including cover sheet):

FOR INFORMATION, CALL:

AT:

FAX NUMBER:

We may be sticking our neck out...

but we'd like your reaction to our service.

TO:

FROM:

PAGES (including cover sheet):

FOR INFORMATION, CALL:

AT:

FAX NUMBER:

We like to think our service is tailored to suit your needs. Should we alter anything?

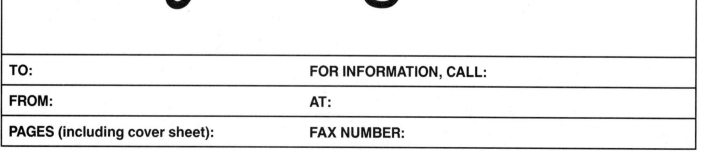

TO:

FOR INFORMATION, CALL:

FROM:

AT:

PAGES (including cover sheet):

FAX NUMBER:

NICE JOB

ON A NEXT-TO-IMPOSSIBLE TASK.

TO:

FROM:

PAGES (including cover sheet):

FOR INFORMATION, CALL:

AT:

FAX NUMBER:

Congratulations!

You worked miracles.

TO: **FOR INFORMATION, CALL:**

FROM: **AT:**

PAGES (including cover sheet):   **FAX NUMBER:**

Congratulations!

Welcome to the fray!

TO:	FOR INFORMATION, CALL:
FROM:	AT:
PAGES (including cover sheet):	FAX NUMBER:

Congratulations!

Looks like your time has finally come!

TO:

FOR INFORMATION, CALL:

FROM:

AT:

PAGES (including cover sheet):

FAX NUMBER:

GOOD LUCK ON THE NEW ENTERPRISE!

TO:

FROM:

PAGES (including cover sheet):

FOR INFORMATION, CALL:

AT:

FAX NUMBER:

YOU'LL BE HAPPY TO KNOW...

MY EXPENSES ARE RIGHT ON TRACK.

TO:

FOR INFORMATION, CALL:

FROM:

AT:

PAGES (including cover sheet):

FAX NUMBER:

COVER SHEET

TO:	FOR INFORMATION, CALL:
FROM:	AT:
PAGES (including cover sheet):	FAX NUMBER:

My entire message is printed below!

Now I know we're on the same page.

TO: **FOR INFORMATION, CALL:**

FROM: **AT:**

PAGES (including cover sheet):   **FAX NUMBER:**

COMPANY FAXES RELEVANT NEWS STORY TO SPECIAL CUSTOMER!!!

TO: **FOR INFORMATION, CALL:**

FROM: **AT:**

PAGES (including cover sheet):   **FAX NUMBER:**

IN CASE YOU MISSED THE ENCLOSED ITEM ABOUT US...

TO: | **FOR INFORMATION, CALL:**

FROM: | **AT:**

PAGES (including cover sheet): | **FAX NUMBER:**

I've decided to take some time off.

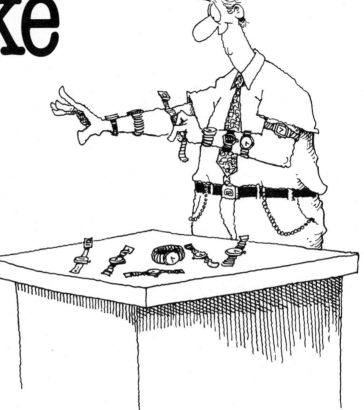

Watch for my return.

TO:

FOR INFORMATION, CALL:

FROM:

AT:

PAGES (including cover sheet):

FAX NUMBER:

Time to recharge my batteries!

See you after vacation.

TO:	FOR INFORMATION, CALL:
FROM:	AT:
PAGES (including cover sheet):	FAX NUMBER:

In case you missed our latest move...

here's our new location.

TO:	FOR INFORMATION, CALL:
FROM:	AT:
PAGES (including cover sheet):	FAX NUMBER: